Respiratory Therapists

Careers in Healthcare

Athletic Trainers
Clinical & Medical Laboratory Scientists
Dental Hygienists
Dietician Nutritionists
EMTs & Paramedics
Nurses
Occupational Therapists
Orthotists & Prosthetists
Physical Therapists
Physician Assistants
Respiratory Therapists
Speech Pathologists & Audiologists
Ultrasound Technicians

CAREERS IN
HEALTHCARE

Respiratory Therapists

Jennifer Hunsaker

MASON CREST
PHILADELPHIA

Mason Crest
450 Parkway Drive, Suite D
Broomall, PA 19008
www.masoncrest.com

©2018 by Mason Crest, an imprint of National Highlights, Inc.

Printed and bound in the United States of America.

CPSIA Compliance Information: Batch #CHC2017.
For further information, contact Mason Crest at 1-866-MCP-Book.

First printing
1 3 5 7 9 8 6 4 2

Library of Congress Cataloging-in-Publication Data

   on file at the Library of Congress
        ISBN: 978-1-4222-3805-9 (hc)
        ISBN: 978-1-4222-7993-9 (ebook)

Careers in Healthcare series ISBN: 978-1-4222-3794-6

QR CODES AND LINKS TO THIRD-PARTY CONTENT

Table of Contents

KEY ICONS TO LOOK FOR:

Words to understand: These words with their easy-to-understand definitions will increase the reader's understanding of the text while building vocabulary skills.

Sidebars: This boxed material within the main text allows readers to build knowledge, gain insights, explore possibilities, and broaden their perspectives by weaving together additional information to provide realistic and holistic perspectives.

Educational Videos: Readers can view videos by scanning our QR codes, providing them with additional educational content to supplement the text. Examples include news coverage, moments in history, speeches, iconic sports moments and much more!

Text-dependent questions: These questions send the reader back to the text for more careful attention to the evidence presented there.

Research projects: Readers are pointed toward areas of further inquiry connected to each chapter. Suggestions are provided for projects that encourage deeper research and analysis.

Series glossary of key terms: This back-of-the book glossary contains terminology used throughout this series. Words found here increase the reader's ability to read and comprehend higher-level books and articles in this field.

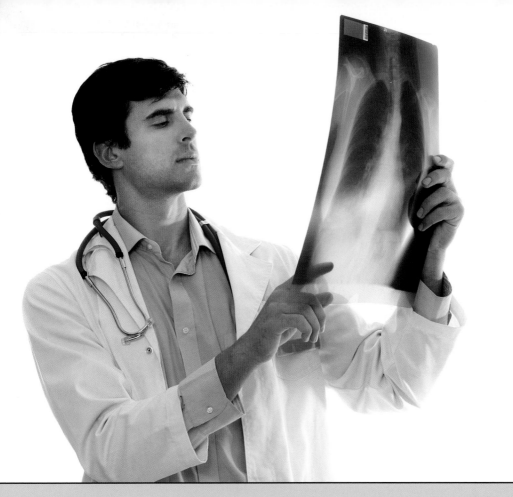

Because a respiratory therapist is the breathing expert in the hospital, many doctors look to them for help with diagnosing and treating breathing problems.

Words to Understand in This Chapter

acute—referring to a medical condition or illness that lasts a short time.

chronic—referring to a medical condition or illness that lasts a long time or keeps coming back.

diagnose—to identify an illness or other medical condition.

protocols—official procedures or rules to follow.

respiratory—referring to the system of the body that controls breathing.

trauma—physical injury or a deeply distressing occurrence.

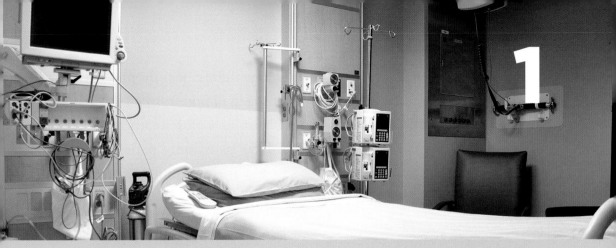

1

What Do Respiratory Therapists Do?

Take a deep breath. Feel the air rushing into your lungs, filling you with energy and life. Now imagine not being able to do that. According to the scientists, the average human takes between 17,280 and 23,040 breaths a day, or more than 6.3 million breaths per year. One of the most basic human functions, breathing delivers oxygen to every organ in the body while simultaneously removing harmful by-products, such as carbon dioxide, from the system. We may not even notice that we are breathing for the majority of our lives, but when something begins to interfere with the way we breathe, it quickly becomes the only thing we can think about.

How Respiratory Therapists Help

Often confused with nurses, *respiratory* therapists (RTs) are health care specialists who focus exclusively on helping patients get the vital oxygen they need to maintain healthy, productive lives. Working closely with doctors, RTs help *diagnose*, treat, and educate patients with asthma, *chronic* obstructive pulmonary disorder (COPD), and other respiratory disorders. In treating patients from premature infants to the elderly, RTs use their intuition, creativity, and knowledge to help patients of all ages breathe more easily.

Consultation

An RT's interaction with a patient begins with a consultation. This process may take place in a number of settings. For premature infants, the consultation process occurs immediately after birth, when infants are examined to determine whether they need assistance breathing. For children and young who have been in an accident or experienced some sort of *trauma*, consultation may happen at the sight of an accident if an RT is on an advance trauma team, or when the patient reaches the emergency room. In patients who have chronic medical conditions, an RT's consultation may happen at a doctor's office or in an outpatient clinic. Regardless of the setting or the patient, the initial consultation involves a three step process—taking a patient history, conducting an assessment, and making a diagnosis.

Patient History

One of the most important aspects of medical care is taking a detailed and accurate patient history. By the time an RT consults with a patient, she or a family member has often given a history to a nurse or another medical assistant. However, there is still a lot of information to be gained by asking questions. No other health care professional has the level of expertise in breathing that an RT does. As an expert in respiratory care, an RT often asks detailed questions about a person's breathing that a doctor or nurse may overlook. During these conversations, RTs can identify significant illnesses, a family medical history, or past illnesses that a patient may have had that may be contributing to her current condition.

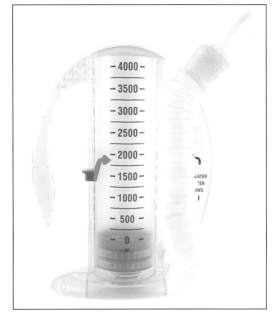

Respiratory therapists use a variety of tools to help patients breathe easier.

Conducting an Assessment

Once the RT has taken a patient's history and asked all the pertinent questions, it is time to conduct an assessment. RTs may use equipment to measure a patient's lung capacity, respiration rate, and oxygen levels in his blood. They will make note in the patient's chart of what they find and use this information as a baseline for treatment. Since medical technology is constantly advancing, the process of assessing patients is also constantly evolving. It is an RT's responsibility to stay up-to-date on all the latest *protocols* to give their patients the best possible care.

Diagnosis

Once RTs have gathered all the necessary information, they are able to make a diagnosis. The patient's diagnosis will largely determine the types of treatment she receives. The diagnosis must be accurate and supported by appropriate information

A Patient I Will Never Forget

A respiratory therapist working in the field told this story about one patient whose story will stay with him forever:

"The hospital where I was working at the time was a level one trauma facility. That meant we got the people in the worst shape—those who could not be handled at other nearby hospitals. One night we had a patient who had been involved in a car accident after a high-speed chase with the police.

"When he arrived, he had been breathing on his own but you could tell by the bruising on his body that had not been wearing a seat belt. I was set up with an intubation tray and took over administering oxygen while the trauma team started assessing him. He was unconscious and I was by his head when suddenly he woke up and started trying to fight the doctors and nurses who were helping him. He didn't know what was happening and he was scared. I tried to keep oxygen on him and he kept trying to push the mask away from his face while swinging at anyone who was around him.

Then, just as suddenly as he started swinging he was unconscious again and stopped breathing. I assisted the doctor with the intubation and then kept bagging him while they tried to get his pulse back. He ended up not making it, because his injuries were too severe. I found out later that he was running from the police because he had run a red light. The police tried to pull him over, but he had almost five pounds of meth in his backseat."

gathered from the patient's history and any testing that was performed. Even doctors look to RTs as respiratory experts and trust them to make accurate judgments of what disease or condition a patient has and the types of treatments she needs.

Treatment

Once a patient has been evaluated, it is important to begin treatment to help the patient breathe more easily. The types of treatment RTs provide for their patients can be divided into two types—rapid-response care and long-term case management.

When a patient has an *acute* problem that prevents him

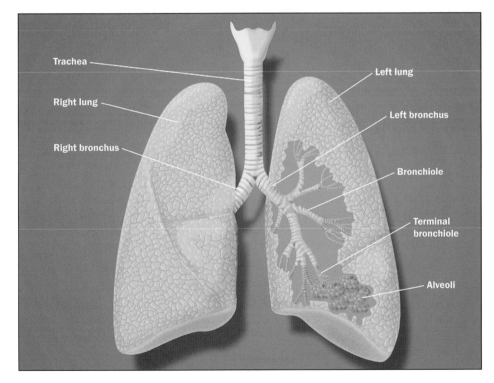

The respiratory system consists of the lungs, trachea, bronchi and diaphragm.

A patient describes her breathing difficulties to a respiratory therapist.

from breathing the way he should, an RT offers something called rapid-response care. During rapid-response care, specialists such as physicians, nurses, and RTs work to stabilize the patient's condition. In hospitals, the call for "code blue" means someone is not breathing or is having a heart attack. RTs would then stop what they are doing and rush to the bedside of that patient. They would then be responsible for helping to clear the patient's airway, providing oxygen to the brain. In premature infants, RTs are responsible for helping babies breathe with as little effort as possible and then gradually weaning them off machines and oxygen until they can breathe on their own. RTs may also be included on rapid-response teams in hospitals where they respond to gravely ill patients before they stop breathing or have a heart attack. In every case, RTs look at the patient's history, conduct an assessment, and provide treatment. They will then check to make sure the treatment is having the desired effect and make notes in the patient's chart.

Educational Video

Scan here for a video that shows what a respiratory therapist does:

RTs also work in outpatient clinics, where they provide long-term case management for patients with chronic breathing problems. These problems can be caused by disease or other chronic conditions, such as asthma or COPD. RTs also work on the medical team treating patients with cancer or other diseases where the patient's ability to breathe might be compromised.

Long-term case management is not as fast-paced as rapid-response care, but it allows RTs to develop relationships with their patients that are not possible during emergency situations. The process is the same for long-term case management, but rather than happening in a short cycle, it happens in longer cycles. For instance, in long-term case management, the goals of care may change over time and with the patient's improvement. As a result, the RT will assess and treat a patient, then reassess, set new goals for the patient's progress, and continue treating the patient. In acute care, the ultimate goal is always

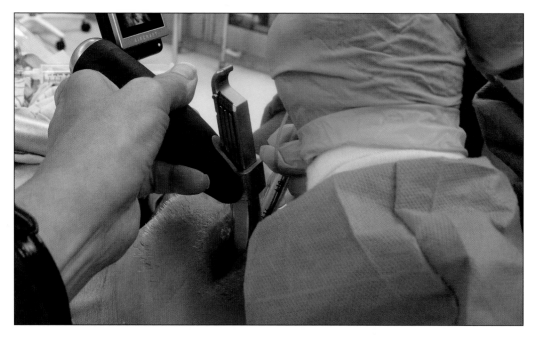

Respiratory therapists are a vital part of the emergency room team.

the same—to help the patient return home as quickly and safely as possible.

Patient Education

Most people do not have the luxury of having a doctor, nurse, respiratory therapist, and nutritionist on staff at home to watch over them all day, every day. Like many other health care professionals, RTs have a responsibility to teach their patients how to manage their conditions on their own. The type of patient education the RT provides will largely depend on the type of condition the patient has. It may be something as simple as teaching a child how to use an asthma inhaler, helping people with COPD understand how their condition will affect exercise, or offering ways to manage a chronic condition such as cystic fibrosis. In every case, the RT must be well-versed in the equipment the patient has, the types of medication she is taking, and any habits that might be affecting the treatment's effectiveness. The RT must also be able to talk to the patient in terms she can understand and have compassion with a patient who may struggle to understand what is happening or what she needs to do. Patient education, regardless of who is conducting it, requires a tremendous amount of patience and tests a professional's knowledge of why she is asking her patients to do the things they need to do.

 Text-Dependent Questions

1. Why would taking a patient's history be a vital part of the diagnostic process?
2. Why is it important for an RT to remain current on all the latest information in medical science?
3. What is the difference between rapid-response care and long-term case management?

Research Project

Talk to a friend or family member who has asthma, COPD, or another chronic respiratory problem. Ask her if she has been treated by a respiratory therapist. What was her experience like? What did the respiratory therapist do? How did the RT help her?

Many respiratory therapists who work in doctors' offices or clinics help patients with chronic breathing problems to manage their condition.

Words to Understand in This Chapter

entrepreneurs—people who start their own business aimed at filling a need in the marketplace.

neonatal—referring to newborn children.

outpatient clinic—a place where a patient receives treatment without being admitted overnight.

rehabilitation facility—an inpatient facility where patients live while receiving medical care aimed at returning them to their home and independent living.

skilled nursing facility—an inpatient facility where patients live while receiving medical care that is aimed at maintaining their quality of life, but not returning the patient home to independent living.

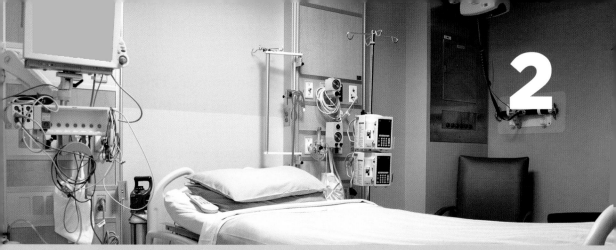

2

A Look at the Opportunities

The Centers for Disease Control and Prevention (CDC) estimate that nearly 15 million adults in the United States live with some form of chronic respiratory disease. These conditions may be caused by smoking, obesity, exposure to toxic chemicals or other harmful substances, genetics, or aging. With a large population of adults nearing or in retirement, called baby boomers, the number of people with chronic breathing problems is expected to rise dramatically in the next three to five years. These people will require medical care provided by qualified, competent respiratory therapists in hospitals, *outpatient clinics*, and other settings.

The U.S. Department of Labor's Bureau of Labor Statistics projects an expected 12 percent increase in the number of RT jobs in the United States over the next decade, meaning the profession is growing much faster than average. This means there will be more than 14,000 new RT jobs over the next ten years. What respiratory therapists do on a daily basis and what they are paid largely depends on where they work.

Settings

Of the more than 120,000 respiratory therapist jobs in the United States in 2014, four out of five worked in hospitals, where RTs attend to the rapid-response and acute-care needs of their patients. The rest work in doctors' offices and outpatient clinics, *rehabilitation* and *skilled nursing facilities*, and for home health care companies providing their patients with more long-term case management.

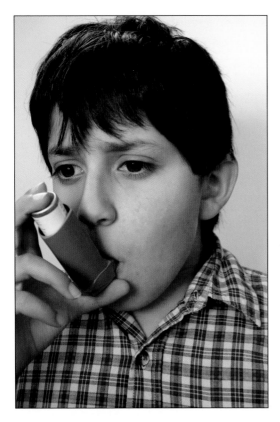

The goal of any respiratory therapist is to teach the patient, no matter how young they are, how to care for themselves.

Hospitals

The majority of acute care in this country takes place in hospitals. As a result, RTs who work in hospitals find themselves working typical hospital schedules. In most cases, these schedules involve three to four 12-hour shifts, covering nights, weekends, and holidays. Hospital RTs work closely with doctors, nurses, physician assistants, surgeons, and other medical professionals to care for their patients. They are required to be on their feet for long periods, often helping to move or turn disabled patients. RTs should be in good physical condition to perform all the duties required of them.

While there are a lot of physical demands associated with working in a hospital, there are rewards as well. Hospitals provide a constant turnover of patients, giving RTs a chance to test their skills all sorts of situations. From medical cases to surgical cases, trauma to intensive care, *neonatal* to labor and delivery, RTs can work in every area of the hospital, often with a variety of other professionals. Among the more common places RTs are found in the hospital are:

- In emergency rooms or with trauma teams, administering lifesaving breathing treatments.
- In neonatal units, helping premature infants breathe without expending too much energy.
- In intensive care units, with gravely ill patients who are on ventilators that keep them alive.
- In pediatric units or even in pediatric hospitals, helping kids with conditions including asthma, cystic fibrosis, or even cancer.
- With anesthesiologists in operating rooms, maintaining a patient's airway so surgeons can focus on the necessary procedure.

The range of their day-to-day activities, along with the sheer volume of people they are able to help, gives hospital-

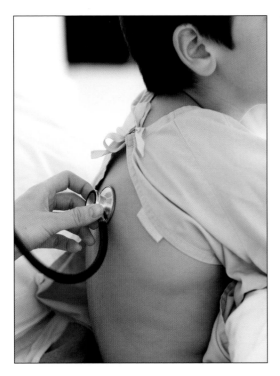

In a hospital setting, respiratory therapists assist with the diagnosis of a variety of breathing problems.

based RTs a sense of satisfaction that they cannot duplicate in other settings.

Outpatient Facilities

Less commonly, RTs work with doctors and nurses in outpatient facilities. In these settings, the RT may be asked to manage the long-term respiratory needs of patients with chronic breathing problems. An RT will work with the same patients over a long period, setting goals for each one's progress. They will then treat the patients with an eye on the patients' long-term goals. The pace of outpatient clinics is significantly slower than that in hospitals, but there are rewards to working in a clinic that are not available in hospitals. RTs have an opportunity to develop relationships with their patients and follow their progress over time. They are also able to maintain hours associated with a clinic that may not require evenings, weekends, or holidays.

Rehabilitation and Skilled Nursing Facilities

The goal of patients in a hospital setting is to be able to return to their home safely and quickly. Those who are unable to care for themselves or who require additional long-term medical care are often moved to a rehabilitation facility. Rehabilitation facilities provide round-the-clock care and therapies that are designed to help patients regain their ability to function and return home as soon as they are safely able to do so. RTs in rehabilitation facilities work with patients who are having difficulty breathing to help them regain their abilities and restore their independence.

Over time, if patients are unable to care for themselves or if their condition worsens, they may be taken to a skilled nursing facility. Skilled nursing facilities, also known as nursing homes, are designed to provide round-the-clock medical care at a variety of levels. Medical professionals may offer physical therapy, occupational therapy, or respiratory therapy to help patients maintain their function, but without the end goal of returning them to their homes. These patients may be elderly, in the final stages of their lives, or unable to physically or mentally care for themselves. In skilled nursing facilities RTs help patients breathe comfortably throughout the remainder of their lives.

Did You Know?

Actively listening to doctors, nurses, medical assistants, and patients is considered one of an RT's most important skills. Not only does it convey respect to the speaker, it ensures that the RT accurately understands the needs of the patient, the work being done by the rest of the health care team, and the urgency of the medical situation.

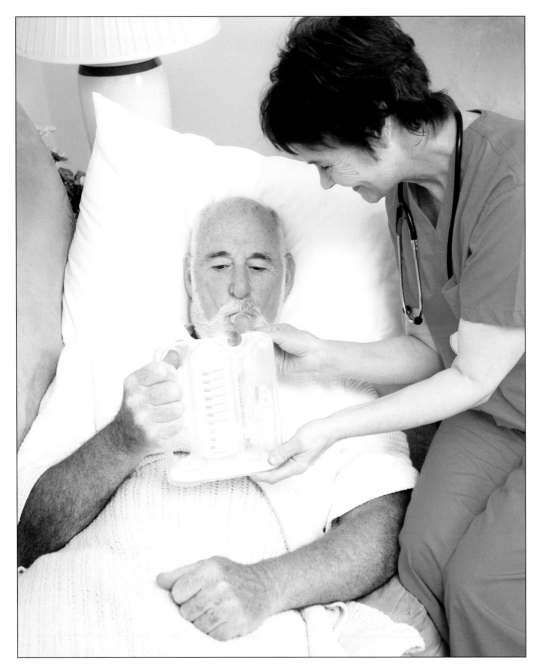

Respiratory therapists often work in nursing homes and skilled nursing facilities, helping patients breathe better.

Home Health Care

People who are unable to go to an outpatient clinic, who are receiving end-of-life hospice care, or who are temporarily homebound may also require the services of an RT. These professionals work with home health care services to attend to a patient's needs in the comfort of her own home. They may teach parents of a chronically ill or premature child how to maintain the child's oxygen levels and how to work the machine that provides the oxygen. They may give breathing treatments to patients recovering from pneumonia and then teach the patients how to use a nebulizer or an inhaler. In every home health care situation, RTs must use their ingenuity and expertise to meet the needs of the patient without the equipment of a hospital at their disposal.

Educational Video

To hear a respiratory therapist talk about this career, scan here:

Salary

A respiratory therapist's median annual salary was approximately $57,800 in May 2015. The lowest 10 percent earned an annual salary of less than $41,000 while the highest earners made more than $80,000. The average salary for an RT working in a hospital is around $59,600, with RTs working in specialty hospitals, such as psychiatric or drug treatment centers, earning an average of nearly $60,500. RTs who work in skilled nursing facilities make an average of $60,200 a year while

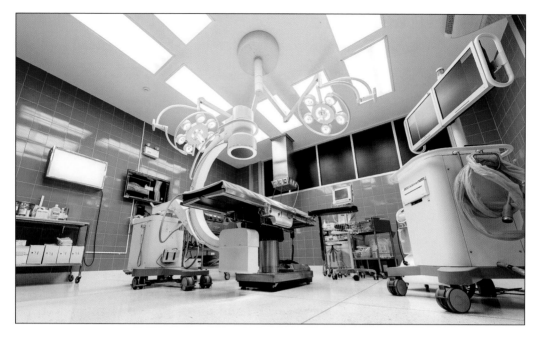

The majority of respiratory therapists work in a hospital setting.

those working in doctor's offices take home an average of $60,600 annually. Finally, those working in home health care make an average of about $54,500 per year. California, Texas, and Florida employ the most RTs while the highest-paid RTs work in California, New Jersey, and Alaska.

Opportunities for Advancement

While you may remain in patient care as a staff RT for your entire career, respiratory therapists often find themselves moving through a hospital's ranks until they are managing other RTs or even entire departments of a hospital. Some become *entrepreneurs*, establishing their own home respiratory care companies that give patients access to equipment and services from the comfort of the patients' own homes. Some even venture into research and design, working with medical technology companies to create better equipment for other RTs to use. Still others become teachers of new RTs or use their expertise to research new protocols for patient care.

 Text-Dependent Questions

1. What are some important things to consider as an RT working in a hospital?
2. What are some advantages of working in an outpatient facility?
3. Which RTs have the highest average salaries? The lowest?

Research Project

Look at the Bureau of Labor Statistics website for your area to find out what an RT will make in a hospital, an outpatient clinic, a rehabilitation facility, and a skilled nursing facility. Then, look at job search websites for your area. Do the statistics match what is currently being offered? How many jobs are available? Where are the majority of the jobs located? Next, pick a location where you would like to work as an RT. Compare the Bureau of Labor Statistics information with the job site information in your desired location. What do you think causes differences in salary, available jobs, and locations where RTs are in demand?

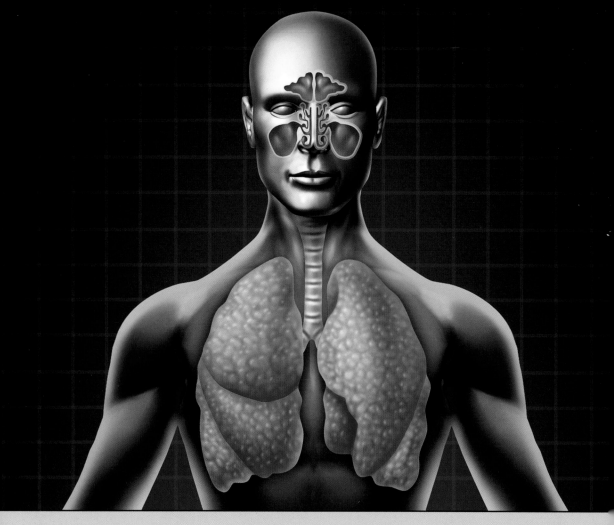

Respiratory therapy students take several courses in anatomy and physiology, including classes about the anatomy and physiology of the respiratory system.

📖 Words to Understand in This Chapter

accredited—referring to an officially authorized or recognized program.

continuing education—opportunities to learn more about the job skills needed to remain current in the field after you have completed your formal education.

credential—a designation by a governing board that the person has skills to perform a particular job.

licensure—the process of becoming officially recognized as having the skills and knowledge to perform a particular job.

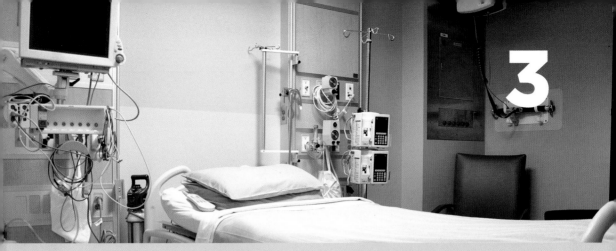

3

Education and Training

Respiratory therapists are viewed as the foremost experts in the body's ability to breathe. Doctors with many years of education and experience look to RTs for their distinctive ability to diagnose and treat a patient's breathing problems. What is surprising is that in order to become a respiratory therapist, a person only needs an associate's degree from an *accredited* program, to pass a board certification exam, and to obtain state *licensure*.

Education

To become an RT, you must first obtain an associate's degree from an accredited program. This means the college or university has gone through a process to prove to the Commission on

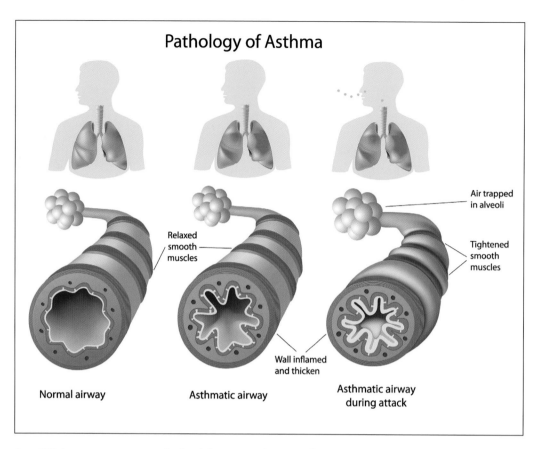

Pathology of Asthma

Air trapped in alveoli

Relaxed smooth muscles

Tightened smooth muscles

Wall inflamed and thicken

Normal airway

Asthmatic airway

Asthmatic airway during attack

In addition to anatomy and physiology, respiratory therapy students have to understand how to diagnose and treat the most common chronic breathing conditions.

Accreditation for Respiratory Care (CoARC) that the higher education institution is giving students the right preparation to become respiratory therapists. This designation is also important for students, since they will not be allowed to sit for *credentialing* exams unless their degree has come from an approved program.

An associate's degree is generally designed to be completed in two academic years, however with clinical components and additional classes, RT students can expect to complete their associate's degree in two calendar years. Students take classes in human anatomy and physiology, pharmacology, the respiratory system, diagnosis of respiratory disorders, and treatment of respiratory disorders, along with math, English, and statistics. They are also required to complete clinical classes where they learn how to do the things an RT does. In a controlled environment, with supervision, while working on mannequins, RT students learn how to give more invasive treatments to patients without causing damage to a human body. They then move on to practicing their clinical skills on people in real-world settings.

Educational Video

Scan here for a look at what it takes to become a respiratory therapist:

Just because an RT needs an associate's degree to provide patient care, doesn't mean all RTs limit their education to a two-year degree. In fact, most RTs hold a minimum of a bachelor's degree in respiratory therapy and many who move on to research or administration obtain master's degrees in the field. Most supervisory jobs require further education beyond an associate's degree and many RTs find that once they have been working for several years their *continuing education* credits can add up to a bachelor's degree. Again, it is important to carefully choose the college or university you will attend, as some offer classes that are only transferrable to their own degree programs, and not to other colleges or universities.

Certification

Once you have completed your associate's degree, you are ready to take the National Board for Respiratory Care exam, called the Therapist Multiple Choice Exam (TMC). This 140-question, multiple-choice test is designed to measure the knowledge and skills of potential RTs by testing them on things an entry-level RT should know. If they pass the test, they are then awarded the certified respiratory therapist (CRT) credential. However, if they score high enough on the test, they not only earn the CRT credential, they are then eligible to take a clinical simulation examination. If they pass this 22-problem test, they then receive the registered respiratory therapist (RRT) credential, considered in the industry to be the "standard of excellence." RTs who receive their CRT have three years to earn their RRT or they are required to take the board certification tests again from the beginning.

Did You Know?

An RT who earns her CRT certification has only three years to earn her RRT certification. Considered to be the gold standard in RT certifications, the RRT shows that a person not only has the basic skills to provide respiratory therapy, but she has demonstrated those skills in a clinical test.

Licensure

After RTs earn their certification, they are required to register for licensure in the state where they will practice. Newly certified CRTs or RRTs will be able to obtain state licensure by registering with the state board of medicine in the state where they plan to practice. However, in order to keep that licensure

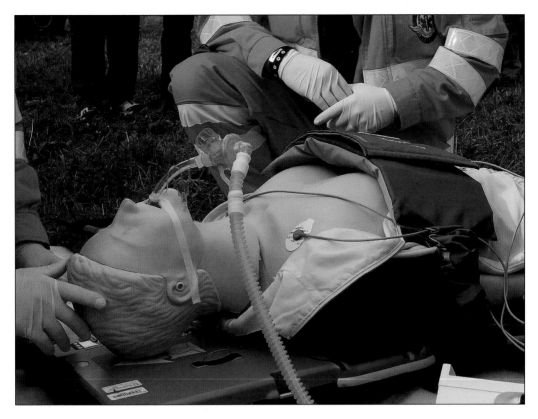

Before they can practice on people, students must first master their techniques on life-like mannequins.

current, many states require RTs to take continuing education credits. These credits can be obtained through classes on a college or university campus, by attending conferences on respiratory therapy, or via online courses designed to teach new skills. Not only does this process help RTs remain current on the latest skills and technology in their field, many RTs use this opportunity to earn credits toward advanced degrees. Continuing education credits required for state licensure vary from state to state. While some may not require continuing

Respiratory therapy students learn how to insert a tube into a patient's trachea to help them breathe, a process called intubation.

education at all, other states require 15–20 hours a year in order to remain current.

Specialty Credentials

Once RTs have earned their basic certification, they can go on to obtain a variety of specialty credentials. These specialties offer RTs opportunities that may be otherwise unavailable to them.

PULMONARY FUNCTION TECHNOLOGISTS (CPFT)/ADVANCED PULMONARY FUNCTION TECHNOLOGISTS (RPFT): While these credentials are technically separate, they are awarded based on an RT's performance on one credential exam. If RTs score high

A Therapist's Educational Advice

A student in a respiratory therapist program took a few moments to describe her education:

"My first classes were in anatomy and physiology with an emphasis in the cardiopulmonary system. Having never taken anatomy and physiology before, they were tough, but I was interested in what I was studying. The next classes in pharmacology and patient assessment really threw me for a loop. I had done well in high school, but I was so frustrated that I wasn't learning what I needed to learn fast enough that I decided to go into something else. After a year of studying psychology, I realized that respiratory therapy really was where I wanted to be. By then, I had gotten familiar with how college classes work, how to study away from class, and how to make the most of what I was learning. Now, I am getting ready to graduate and I am excited to get out into the field and begin helping people.

"My advice to students looking to go into respiratory therapy would be to take as many science classes as you can while you are in high school. Study chemistry and biology. Take human anatomy if it is offered. It gives you a foundation so when you get into college you aren't thrown in the deep end of the pool. It will also help you figure out how you study and memorize best. That way, when it comes time to take something like pharmacology or evaluation processes you aren't trying to learn how to learn."

on the exam, they are awarded the RPFT credential. If they simply pass the exam, they are awarded the CPFT credential. Both credentials show that an RT has the ability to perform the tasks that are required of a pulmonary function technologist.

ADULT CRITICAL CARE SPECIALTY (ACCS) CREDENTIAL: This credential is for RTs who have the RRT credential and experience in working with adults requiring critical care. This may include intensive care units, emergency rooms, and trauma situations. Eligible RTs will have advanced knowledge in the field and pass an exam focusing on the things an RT in adult critical care would know.

NEONATAL/PEDIATRIC SPECIALTY (NPS) CREDENTIAL: This credential is available to RTs who have the RRT credential or the CRT credential and more than one year of experience in neonatal or pediatric settings. This exam has 140 multiple-choice questions that focus on clinical data, equipment used in these settings, and procedures that are used in treating infants and children.

SLEEP DISORDERS SPECIALTY (SDS) CREDENTIAL: This credential is available to RTs who have the RRT credential or the CRT credential and more than one year of experience working with patients who have sleep disorders. The exam focuses on the information an RT would only be able to gain while working with patients who have sleep disorders.

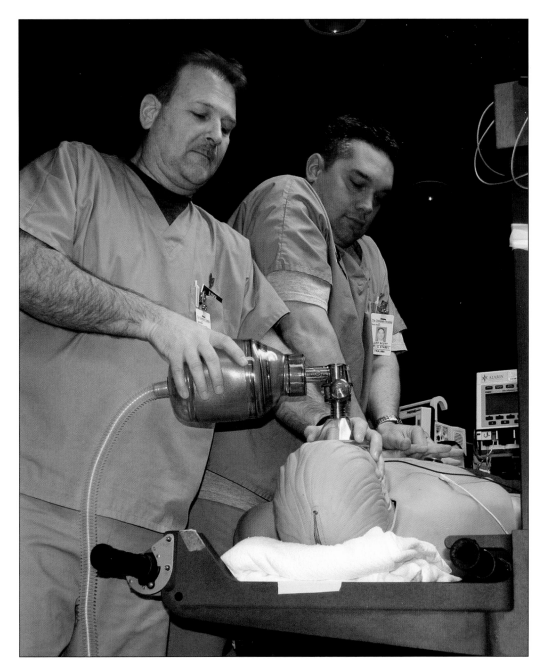

Working together, respiratory therapy students learn what to do when a patient stops breathing entirely.

Which Respiratory Therapy Program Is Right for You?

RT programs are generally competitive to get into and widely offered at technical colleges, community colleges, and even universities. However, choosing the right one for you may prove to be more complicated than simply picking one out of a catalog. Since many RTs continue their education beyond an associate's degree, look for a school whose credits are transferable to another college or university. Many for-profit, technical colleges offer classes that are only transferrable to their own for-profit technical colleges. This means that if you receive your associate's degree from one of these schools you may have to repeat classes at another college or university offering a bachelor's degree in the same field.

The University of Minnesota-Twin Cities has one of the highest-ranked programs for respiratory therapists in the country.

It is also important to consider colleges or universities that have a high first-time pass rate on the TMC exam. This means the education they are offering is effectively teaching RTs what they need to know to work in the field. Look at the admission rate versus the application rate to see how competitive the program is. Additionally, you will need to factor into your decision the costs of living at home or away from home, whether you want to have a university or technical college experience, whether you will be working while you attend school, and the costs of tuition and fees. In the end, selecting the right school for you is a process that begins and ends with research.

 ## Text-Dependent Questions

1. Why do many RTs go on to receive advanced degrees?
2. What is the difference between CRT and RRT certification?
3. What factors are important to consider when choosing an RT school?

 ## Research Project

Make a chart of accredited respiratory therapy programs in your area. Include information like location, tuition costs, number of students admitted, number of students who graduate, number of students who pass the national board exam on their first attempt, and financial aid available. Be sure to include information on whether credits are transferable to another university to continue your education. Many applied technology programs do not offer credits that are transferable to a standard university, where you would be able to finish a bachelor's degree.

Few inventions have revolutionized respiratory therapy the way the inhaler has. It is a simple machine that delivers targeted medicine when the patient needs it.

📖 Words to Understand in This Chapter

bronchial—related to the lungs; the bronchi are tubes that carry air into the lungs.

canister—a round or cylindrical container, typically one made of metal, used for storing things.

catheter—a flexible tube inserted through a narrow opening into a body cavity, particularly the bladder, for removing fluid.

inhalation—the act of breathing in.

secretions—substances discharged by a gland, an organ, or a cell in the body for a particular purpose.

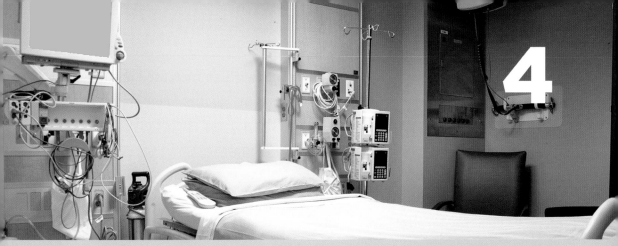

A Look Back
and a Look Ahead

R espiratory therapy is an exciting field, often on the cutting edge of technological advances in medicine. If a patient does not have the ability to keep oxygen flowing to the brain, all other medical procedures are pretty pointless. However, respiratory therapy was not always a haven for technological advancement. In fact, it was not always a profession on its own.

A Look Back

While the respiratory therapy profession dates back to the 1940s, research into respiratory care dates back to the early 1900s. In its early years, so-called "oxygen orderlies" would spend their time moving large canisters of compressed oxygen from one patient to the next. They would either use nasal catheters or tents to provide patients with an increased level of oxygen for a time and then move on to the next patient. Oxygen orderlies were trained on the job and their only duties were administering compressed oxygen.

Considered to be one of the fathers of respiratory therapy, Dr. Edwin R. Levine called attention in his memoirs to the need for respiratory therapy in patients who had just received surgery:

> "I found that post-operative patients needed to be moved to prevent bronchial obstruction. Because of our previous physiologic work with retained secretions, I realized that patients could not remain on their backs during the post-operative period, although nurses insisted on this. I stayed with every patient, making sure that the operative side stayed dependent most of the time, but still moving the patient around. We discovered that the important part of thoracic surgery was not so much what was done on the operating table, but what was done to prevent post-operative pneumonia by controlling secretions and breathing.
>
> "When I became an attending physician, I insisted that the residents follow cases. We were able to handle some of the patients much better. In general, though, I was still dissatisfied. It was necessary that when these patients received respiratory therapy they simply had to be supervised. I was able to have the residents supervise some of this; the nurses were trained a little better; but, the residents were uneven in quality, and the nurses didn't have time to handle all of the situations."

In 1943, Dr. Levine began organizing an inhalation therapy program of sorts to help his patients after surgery. He trained therapists on the job, giving them regular classes on human anatomy, physiology, and the cardiopulmonary system. He also included clinical applications in his program to offer newly trained technicians an opportunity to practice their skills while relieving him of some of his post-surgical duties.

Then, on July 13, 1946, a group of oxygen orderlies, physicians, and nurses, headed by Dr. Levine, met at the University of Chicago and formed the Inhalation Therapy Association (ITA). This was an exciting time in medicine. World War II had ended, the postwar economy had begun to boom, and many veterans had returned home from both fronts with unique medical needs. The urgency in the health care field was palpable, as several new professions emerged. Nine months after the ITA was founded, respiratory therapy as a profession was born on April 15, 1947 when the ITA became a legally chartered organization in Illinois.

At the time, an inhalation therapy department manager was in charge of everything related to respiration in a hospi-

The goal of every respiratory therapist is to help patients live active and healthy lives.

tal. From fixing equipment to planning and budgeting, inhalation therapy department managers were often left to their own devices to run the department and to train other therapists. In 1947, there was no formal educational program designed to train inhalation therapists. This meant those in the field had to rely on their own experience to train others in how to do their jobs. This proved problematic, since the hospital's inhalation therapy services were only as good as the previous therapist. Inhalation therapists who were not familiar with the scientific process, including disproving biases and proving facts, would often develop false ideas that would then be passed on to other therapists.

Forging a Standard in Education

With on-the-job training riddled with incorrect assumptions and therapist biases, a standard of formal education was required in the field. Therapists needed similar training across the country to reliably perform their jobs. In 1950, the New York Academy of Medicine published a report titled, "Standard of Effective Administration of Inhalation Therapy." In the report, several scientists had laid out the appropriate ways to administer inhalation therapy as well as standards for the training and education of the therapists. This report set the stage for the creation of formal educational standards, many of which are

Did You Know?

In 1982, California passed the first law requiring state licensure of respiratory therapists. In honor of this law, President Ronald Reagan proclaimed the fourth week of October the first National Respiratory Care Week. This tradition continues today and raises awareness for improving lung health around the world while shedding light on the respiratory therapy profession.

Several pieces of specialized equipment have come on the market lately that help parents administer breathing medication to infants at home.

still in practice today. However, it was not until May 11, 1954 that the New York State Society of Anesthesiologists and the Medical Society of the State of New York formed a Special Joint Committee in Inhalation Therapy. This task force began establishing the standards for instruction that would govern inhalation therapy schools across the country. A first step toward creating a system of accreditation for inhalation therapy programs, the task force's recommendations would eventually be adopted by the American Medical Association in 1956.

Educational Video

Scan here for history of the respiratory therapy profession:

In the early days of the profession, the majority of inhalation therapists were men. The medical profession as a whole was highly segregated along gender lines. Women tended to be nurses, men tended to be doctors, and unskilled, but strong, men tended to fill an "orderly" role where their primary duties involved lifting patients and carrying heavy equipment. Since the early respiratory therapists were considered "oxygen orderlies," and the compressed oxygen tanks they were forced to carry around were very heavy, the majority of early inhalation therapists were men. However, technological advances in the 1960s and 1970s paved the way for women to enter the field and begin practicing.

A Look to the Future

Even though respiratory therapy has been a recognized profession for more than 70 years, advancement in the profession is by no means over. In 2007, the American Association for Respiratory Care (AARC) began recommending new standards for credentialing and licensing respiratory therapists. One of the association's recommendations was to require a bachelor's degree for entry into the profession by 2015. While this recommendation was rejected by the Commission on Accreditation for Respiratory Care (CoARC), the idea is still under consideration. Many allied health care professions, such as physical therapists, occupational therapists, and even dental hygienists have sought ways to allow patients to have direct access to their care without having to go through physicians or hospitals. Since the vast majority of RTs currently work in hospitals, the idea that patients who have asthma, COPD, or other chronic breathing problems could have direct access to their care seems

A respiratory therapist helps a patient in a hospital.

Since breathing is one of the basic needs of the human body, when someone is unable to breathe or breathing becomes difficult, they find themselves at the emergency room of a hospital where a respiratory therapist can help them.

far off. However, the move toward requiring a bachelor's degree for entry into the profession is one step in that direction.

More and more RTs are pursuing bachelor's and master's degrees on their own after they enter the profession. This not only gives them greater authority, it also creates an interesting ripple effect in the types of jobs that are available to them. Many times, an RT with an associate's degree will have to compete with an RT with a bachelor's degree for the same job. Given the choice, many hospitals and clinics will opt for the RT with the more advanced degree. RTs with associate's degrees will also find that their pay reaches the maximum possible level much faster than those with bachelor's or master's degrees. It would not be surprising if, in the coming years, a bachelor's degree will be considered the minimum degree for entry-level RTs in order to level the playing field when it comes to getting a job after graduation.

Text-Dependent Questions

1. Why were the majority of the first inhalation therapists men?
2. Why did Dr. Edwin R. Levine see the need for respiratory therapy?
3. What impact would requiring a bachelor's degree for entry into the respiratory therapy profession have on the profession?

Research Project

Talk to a respiratory therapist who has been in the profession for several years. Ask him what his first job was like. Ask what he did, how he interacted with doctors and nurses, what courses he was required to take for his education, and how he was treated in the field. Then, ask him to compare the first part of his career with his career today. What has changed? What has stayed the same? Finally, ask him to describe what he feels the future holds for the profession. Many current RTs can paint a fairly accurate picture of what the next five to ten years will be like when you are entering the profession. Based on the RT's answers, how do you think you should gear your education and training?

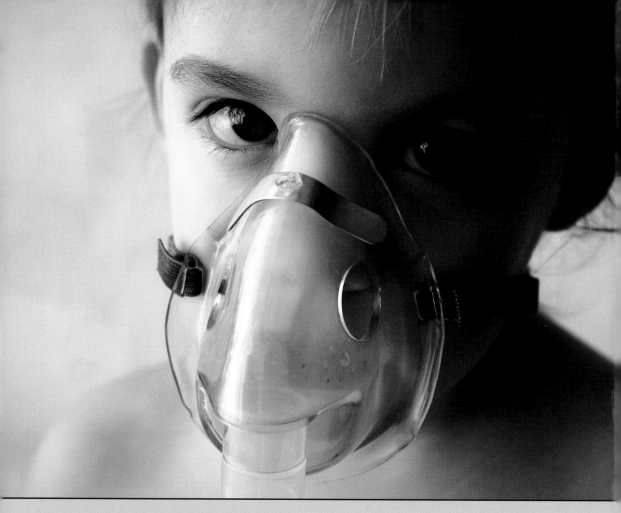

A little girl receives a treatment designed for children with asthma.

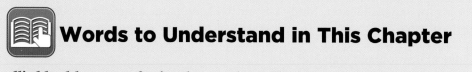 **Words to Understand in This Chapter**

allied health care professionals—members of health care professions who assist physicians in their quest to provide the best possible patient care.

direct care—medical care offered by health care professionals without having to obtain a doctor's authorization.

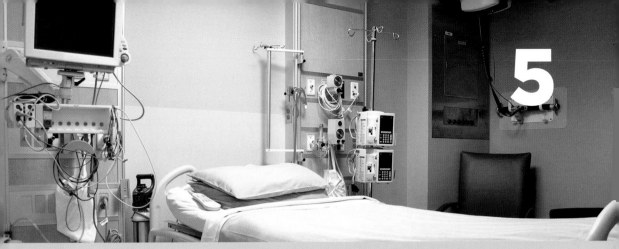

Overview
and Interview

There are currently more than 120,000 practicing respiratory therapists in the United States. Earning an average salary of about $57,800 per year, RTs provide care for patients who are experiencing problems breathing. In treating those with chronic illnesses, such as asthma and COPD, as well as those who have recently had surgery or experienced a trauma, RTs are considered the foremost experts in the respiratory system. This, together with an expected 12 percent increase in demand over the next ten years, gives respiratory therapy the respect it deserves.

According to the Bureau of Labor Statistics, four out of five respiratory therapists work in hospitals. The rest divide their work time between outpatient clinics, doctors' offices, skilled nursing facilities, home health care companies, and companies

Educational Video

Scan here to watch an overview of what respiratory therapists do:

that create new respiratory therapy technology. While the majority of RTs work in hospitals, the highest-paid RTs work in the offices of physicians. With the exception of those who work in home health care, the average annual salary of any of the environments varies by less than $1,000.

Respiratory therapists are required to obtain an associate's degree, pass the Therapist Multiple Choice Examination (TMC), and become licensed in the state where they intend to practice. Once they have received their certified respiratory therapist (CRT) certification, they have three years to obtain their registered respiratory therapist (RRT) certification by taking a second clinical exam. If they are unable to do this in the time allotted, they will need to retake the TMC and the three-year time frame will begin again.

There are a variety of specialty certifications available to those who already have their RRT. These include adult critical care specialty (ACCS), the certification for pulmonary function technologist (CPFT) and registered pulmonary function technologist (RPFT), the neonatal/pediatric specialty (NPS), and the sleep disorders specialty (SDS) credentials. Each credential is available to RRTs who have experience working in that particular area and who can pass an exam geared toward those specialty areas.

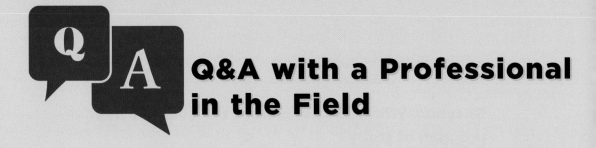

Q&A with a Professional in the Field

Melissa Goss

What follows is transcript from an interview with Melissa Goss, a respiratory therapist in a small, rural hospital.

Question: How long have you been a respiratory therapist?

Melissa: I have been a respiratory therapist since 2013.

Question: What inspired you to get into this field?

Melissa: When I was in high school, my dad was on a ventilator after a surgery that did not go well. After that experience, I thought about going into nursing so I could work with patients who were on life support. One of the first questions they asked when I went to sign up for nursing school was "Why do you want to become a nurse?"

When I told them about my desire to work with patients who are on life support, they informed me that what I was looking for was actually respiratory therapy, not nursing. So, I went into respiratory therapy and never looked back.

Question: What kinds of classes did you take in your program of study?

Melissa: I went to a two-year program in Mesa, Arizona. In order to be a respiratory therapist, you have to have an associate of science degree, but it isn't like a normal AS where you have summers off. Instead, you go the full calendar year for two years. The first year focuses on your general education requirements, like math, English, chemistry, organic chemistry. Then during the second year I started studying things like cardiac anatomy and physiology, cardiopulmonary diseases, and emergency care. What many people don't realize is that we work with both the heart and the lungs. We might perform cardiac stress tests to make sure the heart is healthy and getting the oxygen it demands. We have one particular test that calls for a patient to wear a device for two weeks and then return the device. We then have a record of every heartbeat that has happened for two weeks and can see when the patient has had problems or if her oxygen rates have changed with exercise or activity.

Question: Where did you work when you first graduated?

Melissa: I worked for a larger hospital in Mesa when I first graduated.

Question: Where do you work now?

Melissa: I currently work in a small, rural hospital in the town where I grew up in northern California. It's a town of about 5,000 people so you tend to see the people you treat in the grocery store or the gas station. That presents its own challenges, since you have to separate what you are doing from who you are treating. You might have someone come in suffering acute respiratory distress and have to consciously remove from your mind the fact that you ate Thanksgiving dinner at his house or that you know his family in order to do your job.

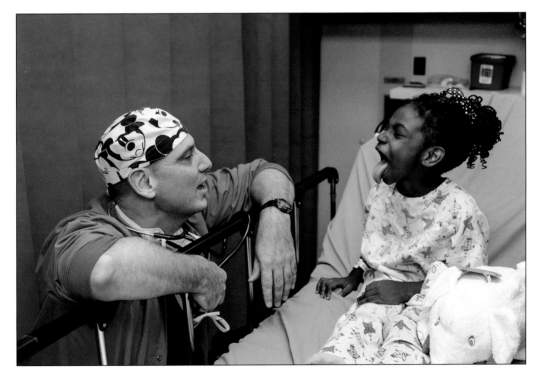

Every year, during cold and flu season thousands of patients nationwide are hospitalized with pneumonia.

Question: What surprised you the most when you first became a respiratory therapist?

Melissa: I had no idea there were so many different aspects of the job. In nursing, you treat the total body, and while you can specialize in intensive care or pediatrics, you have to be able to care for every system in the person's body. You would think in something as specialized as respiratory therapy that focusing on one system would mean you don't ever experience variety. What actually happens is that you get to treat every type of patient in a hospital. When I was working in Mesa, we were present at every caesarian section in case something went wrong with the mother or baby. Now that I am in a smaller hospital, I work in every area of the hospital. Cardiac patients, intensive care, neonatal intensive care, pediatrics, labor and delivery, surgery—we have a hand in all of it.

Question: What is the most rewarding aspect of the job?

Melissa: Seeing someone you treated at her child's soccer game or her grandchild's birthday party. In larger cities, you

Did You Know?

Respiratory therapists are not only concerned with the way the lungs work in the body, they are also concerned that the heart receives enough oxygen to function properly.

don't have that level of contact with the people you treat. I definitely didn't have it when I was working in Mesa, but helping extremely sick people get better and then living their lives is the best part of what I do.

Question: Can you share a memorable experience you had with a patient that will stay with you forever?

Melissa: We have patients that we see regularly, every year. Right now we're in flu and pneumonia season and every year we see one particular patient between January and March. It seems like she regularly ends up on a ventilator for days or weeks at a time. Then, suddenly she will improve. After lying in a bed for up to a month on a ventilator, she will be moved to a rehabilitation center—either for additional respiratory care or just because she is too physically weak to go home. I will see her occasionally in the summer at the grocery store. She knows me by name, she asks about my family, and she always thanks me for helping her.

Question: What kind of personal traits do you think are important for a respiratory therapist?

Melissa: You have to be able to react under pressure. When someone is in trouble and you are there to help intubate, you can't stop and look something up in a book. You have to be able to perfectly recall your training and act on it. The certification exam to receive the RRT is like virtually treating a patient. You leave your keys, your phone, everything with the proctor and go in with a pencil and your identification card. Then, you have to know your formulas well enough to treat a patient without any help. You have to calculate ventilation, respiration, oxygen needs—all of it—without looking at a book or a paper. It's a challenging test, but it mimics what you experience in the real world.

Question: What advice would you give to someone who is considering a career in respiratory therapy?

Melissa: Study hard. You have to be able to recall the things you learned in school at a moment's notice. But your learning doesn't stop with what you learn in the classroom. You have to constantly read journals, take classes, and learn about the latest and best practices in order to stay current. If you love learning, if you want to help people and have a variety of ways you can make an impact, this is the field to choose.

Question: Where do you see the profession in ten years?

Melissa: I have been reading a lot in the professional journals about moving to a more *direct care* approach. Rather than being in hospitals or clinics as *allied health care professionals*, there seems to be growing support for a nurse-practioner level of care. In nursing, nurse-practioners or physician assistants are able to see patients in a clinical setting and provide the care a patient is seeking without the oversight of a physician. It wouldn't surprise me if, in the next ten years, we see more respiratory therapists in private practice where physicians can refer patients to see them for care. What we do is really important in hospitals, but it would give our patients more access to the services we provide.

 Text-Dependent Questions

1. What is one of the personal traits Melanie feels is important to be a successful respiratory therapist?
2. According to Melanie, how does the RRT exam prepare you for situations where you will have to treat patients?
3. What advice does Melanie give to those considering a career in respiratory therapy? Why would the ability to study come into play after graduation?

Research Project

Look into programs in your school that offer classes that might be relevant to respiratory therapy. If possible, take classes in biology, chemistry, human anatomy, or even statistics to prepare for later schooling in a respiratory therapy program.

Series Glossary

accredited—a college or university program that has met all of the requirements put forth by the national organization for that job. The official stamp of approval for a degree.

Allied Health Professions—a group of professionals who use scientific principles to evaluate, diagnose and treat a variety of diseases. They also promote overall wellness and disease prevention in support of a variety of health care settings. (These may include physical therapists, dental hygienists, athletic trainers, audiologists, etc.)

American Medical Association (AMA)—the AMA is a professional group of physicians that publishes research about different areas of medicine. The AMA also advocates for its members to define medical concepts, professions, and recommendations.

anatomy—the study of the structure of living things; a person and/or animal's body.

associate's degree—a degree that is awarded to a student who has completed two years of study at a junior college, college, or university.

bachelor's degree—a degree that is awarded to a student by a college or university, usually after four years of study.

biology—the life processes especially of an organism or group.

chemistry—a science that deals with the composition, structure, and properties of substances and with the transformations that they undergo.

cardiology—the study of the heart and its action and diseases.

cardiopulmonary resuscitation (CPR)—a procedure designed to restore normal breathing after cardiac arrest that includes the clearance of air passages to the lungs, mouth-to-mouth method of artificial respiration, and heart massage by the exertion of pressure on the chest.

Centers for Disease Control—the Centers for Disease Control and Prevention (CDC) is a federal agency that conducts and supports health promotion, prevention and preparedness activities in the United States with the goal of improving overall public health.

diagnosis—to determine what is wrong with a patient. This process is especially important because it will determine the type of treatment the patient receives.

diagnostic testing—any tests performed to help determine a medical diagnosis.

EKG machine—an electrocardiogram (EKG or ECG) is a test that checks for problems with the electrical activity of your heart. An EKG shows the heart's electrical activity as line tracings on paper. The spikes and dips in the tracings are called waves. The heart is a muscular pump made up of four chambers.

first responder—the initial personnel who rush to the scene of an accident or an emergency.

Health Insurance Portability and Accountability Act (HIPAA)—a federal law enacted in 1996 that protects continuity of health coverage when a person changes or loses a job, that limits health-plan exclusions for preexisting medical conditions, that requires that patient medical information be kept private and secure, that standardizes electronic transactions involving health information, and that permits tax deduction of health insurance premiums by the self-employed.

internship—the position of a student or trainee who works in an organization, sometimes without pay, in order to gain work experience or satisfy requirements for a qualification.

kinesiology—the study of the principles of mechanics and anatomy in relation to human movement.

Master of Science degree—a Master of Science is a master's degree in the field of science awarded by universities in many countries, or a person holding such a degree.

obesity—a condition characterized by the excessive accumulation and storage of fat in the body.

pediatrics—the branch of medicine dealing with children.

physiology—a branch of biology that deals with the functions and activities of life or of living matter (as organs, tissues, or cells) and of the physical and chemical phenomena involved.

Surgeon General—the operational head of the US Public Health Department and the leading spokesperson for matters of public health.

Further Reading

Kalanithi, Paul. *When Breath Becomes Air.* Waterville, ME: Thorndike Press, 2016.

Masferrer, R., G. K. Dolan, and J. J. Ward. "History of the Respiratory Care Profession." In G. G. Burton, J. E. Hodgkin, and J. J. Ward, eds., *Respiratory Care: A Guide to Clinical Practice*, 3rd ed., pp. 3–18. Philadelphia: J.B. Lippincott, 1991.

Vranich, Belisa. *Breathe: The Simple, Revolutionary 14-Day Program to Improve Your Mental And Physical Health.* New York: St. Martin's Griffin, 2016.

Internet Resources

www.bls.gov/ooh/healthcare/respiratory-therapists.htm
This government website provides information on
salaries and job outlook for respiratory therapists.

www.aarc.org/careers/what-is-an-rt/advancement-opportunities/
The American Association for Respiratory Care
(AARC) is the leading national and international
professional association for respiratory care. The
AARC encourages and promotes professional excellence, advances the science and practice of respiratory care, and serves as an advocate for patients and
their families, the public, the profession and the respiratory therapist.

www.nbrc.org/rrt/pages/default.aspx
The National Board for Respiratory Care (NBRC) is
a voluntary health-certifying board that was created
in 1960 to evaluate the professional competence of
respiratory therapists.

Index

Numbers in **bold italic** refer to captions.

premature, 8, 12–13, 19
inhalation therapy, 40–44
  See also respiratory therapists
Inhalation Therapy Association (ITA), 41
inhalers, 23, *38*
interview, 51–57
intubation, *32*

Levine, Edwin R., 40–41
licensure, 26, 27, 30–32, 42, 44, 50
  See also education
long-term case management, 11, 13, 18, 20, 21

Medical Society of the State of New York, 43

National Board for Respiratory Care, 30
National Respiratory Care Week, 42
neonatal/pediatric specialty (NPS) credential, 34, 50
New York Academy of Medicine, 42
New York State Society of Anesthesiologists, 43
nursing homes, 21, *22*
  See also skilled nursing facilities

outpatient clinics, 13, 16, 17, 20, 49
oxygen, 7, 8, 9, 12, 23, 39–40, 44, 54
oxygen orderlies, 39–41, 44
  See also respiratory therapists

patient education, 14–15, *18*
pneumonia, 40, *53*
protocols, 6, 9, 25
pulmonary function technologists (CPFT) credential, 32, 50

rapid-response care, 11–13, 18
Reagan, Ronald, 42
registered pulmonary function technologists (RPFT) credential, 32, 50
registered respiratory therapist (RRT) credential, 30, 50
rehabilitation facilities, 16, 18, 20–21
research projects, 15, 25, 37, 47, 57
respiratory disorders, 8, 13, 14–15, *16*, 17, 20, *28*, 45, 49

respiratory system, 11
respiratory therapists
  and assessment conducting, 9, 13
  and career advancement, 24–25
  and career growth, 17, 49
  collaboration of, with doctors, 8, 11, 12, 13, 19, 21, 27
  and consultation, 8
  definition of, 7–8
  and diagnosing, 9, 11
  and education, 26, 27–34, 36–37, 42–43, 44–47, 50, 52
  and future of career, 44–47, 56–57
  gender of, 44
  and history of career, 39–44
  job duties of, 8–9, 11–15, 19–21, 49
  and long-term case management, 11, 13, 18, 20, 21
  number of, 18, 49
  and patient education, 14–15, *18*
  and patient histories, 8–9, 13
  personal experiences of, 10, 33, 51–57
  personal traits of, 54–55
  physical fitness of, 19
  and rapid-response care, 11–13, 18
  salaries of, 23–24, 49–50
  and specialty credentials, 32, 34, 50
  and treatment, 11–13
  and work environments, 8, 10, 12–14, 17, 18–24, 34, 45, 49–50, 53
  and work hours, 18, 20

salaries, respiratory therapist, 23–24, 49–50
skilled nursing facilities, 16, 18, 20–21, *22*, 49
sleep disorders, 34, 50
sleep disorders specialty (SDS) credential, 34, 50
Special Joint Committee in Inhalation Therapy, 43

Therapist Multiple Choice Exam (TMC), 30, 37, 50
  See also education
trauma, 6, 8, 10, 19, 49
treatment, 11–13

World War II, 41

About the Author

Jennifer Hunsaker grew up wanting to become a pediatric surgeon specializing in cleft palate repair. Instead, she earned a Bachelor's Degree in Communicative Disorders and a Master's Degree in Human Resource Management and went on to work as a consultant for small businesses. Unsatisfied by the business world, she returned to her first love as a writer of medically-related content geared toward children, students, and those who work with them. When she isn't writing, she is chasing her husband, four children, and Yorkie named Wookie through the mountains of Northern Utah.

Picture Credits: Alila07 | Dreamstime.com: 28; Baronoskie | Dreamstime.com: 48; Peter Elvidge | Dreamstime: 18; Hdconnelly | Dreamstime.com: 9; Legger | Dreamstime.com: 11; Danijel Micka | Dreamstime.com: 17, 53; Nagy-bagoly Ilona | Dreamstime.com: 38; Photoeuphoria | Dreamstime.com: 41; Robhainer | Dreamstime.com: 43; Showface | Dreamstime.com: 6; Skypixel | Dreamstime.com: 26; Syda Productions | Dreamstime.com: 12; Wavebreakmedia Ltd | Dreamstime.com: 20; Lisa F. Young | Dreamstime.com: 22; courtesy Melissa Goss: 51; used under license from Shutterstock, Inc.: 1, 2, 14, 24, 31, 32, 35, 36, 45, 46.